A

What is Anxiety and Simple Ways to Reduce Anxiety, Social Anxiety, Panic Attacks, and Fear in Order to Master Your Life

Table of Contents

Introduction

I want to thank you and congratulate you for downloading the book, *"Anxiety: What is Anxiety and Simple Ways to Reduce Anxiety, Social Anxiety, Panic Attacks, and Fear in Order to Master Your Life"*. You have taken one giant step toward combating anxiety in your life, and this proves just how strong you are.

This book contains proven steps and strategies on how to overcome the scourge that anxiety has become in today's world. There is no feeling worse than always wanting to run away from yourself and others. You simply don't want to deal with the issues around you and would rather crawl somewhere and hide. This is what anxiety does. It ruins your life.

If you are an anxiety sufferer, it may even be difficult to focus on reading this book. I just want you to know that you are strong enough to overcome anxiety. That is what this book is here for: to help you understand what you are facing and deal with it.

This book will take you through a brief analysis of what anxiety really is so that you have a firm grasp of the enemy you face. Others may not have a deep awareness of what anxiety really is but it is important for you to do so.

We will also discuss the different types and forms of anxiety and how they manifest themselves. As you well know, anxiety is just a generalized term that covers other ailments like panic attacks, social anxiety, and phobias. All these will be unpacked in this book.

Finally, we will walk through some simple steps that you can take starting today to cure yourself of anxiety. We will look at simple breathing and meditation exercises, mindfulness techniques, and some confidence building skills. Maintaining a healthy diet and exercise are also part of the healing process, so we shall go through some of the ways to incorporate them into your daily routine.

I must tell you that the process of healing from anxiety is a long journey that takes time. However, I am confident that you will stay the course until you win your battle. You are worth fighting for, and I hope that by the time you complete this book, you will be well on your way to find your peace, strength, and joy.

Thanks again for downloading this book, I hope you enjoy it!

information is without contract or any type of guarantee assurance.

The trademarks that are used are without any consent, and the publication of the trademark is without permission or backing by the trademark owner. All trademarks and brands within this book are for clarifying purposes only and are the owned by the owners themselves, not affiliated with this document.

Chapter 1: Understanding Anxiety

Life can be extremely unpleasant for someone who suffers from anxiety. You feel as if everybody else is going through and enjoying life, but somehow you are stuck on the other side of the glass, watching and waiting.

The truth is that experiencing occasional anxiety is a normal thing in life. Most people know how to manage it when it creeps up and it doesn't really interfere with their daily lives. However, the anxiety we are talking about is the one that is persistent, overwhelming, and uncontrollable.

The worst part about this anxiety is the self-doubt. You feel confused about why you are the way you are and how long this kind of misery will last. Even your own family members can fail to understand your behavior and look down on your condition. People who don't understand anxiety as a disorder can misdiagnose it as simply stress or shyness. They just cannot understand how terrifying, discomfiting, and all-consuming anxiety can be.

It is at this point that those closest to you become impatient with you and tell you to "Pull yourself together," assuming that you are being selfish and refusing to engage with them during events like birthdays and weddings. People start feeling like you are trying to avoid them, yet on the inside, you are literally screaming out in agony and fear.

All you are looking for is someone who understands you so that you can share with them your sense of helplessness and hopelessness; to tell you that you are not losing your mind and the thoughts in your mind are normal.

If this describes you, I must tell you that you are not crazy and you are not alone. You just suffer from a very common condition known as anxiety disorder.

What is Anxiety?

Anxiety is a medical disorder that is characterized by excessive and irrational fear of normal situations. The fear disables you so much that you cannot even engage in regular activities. This disorder is serious and requires treatment just as any normal physical ailment.

In fact, what most people don't realize is that anxiety disorders are the most pervasive disorders in the USA. More than 40 million men, women, and children suffer from anxiety disorders in the US, but the sad reality is that less than 13 million of anxiety sufferers get treatment for their condition. This shows you just how common it is, so do not feel like you have to go through it alone.

When we talk about an anxiety disorder, we are simply using a general term. Anxiety disorders can manifest themselves as generalized anxiety disorder (GAD), panic attacks, social anxiety disorder, and phobias.

Is It Stress or Anxiety Disorder?

Most people tend to confuse normal anxiety, or stress, with anxiety disorder. They are two totally different things. Here are just a few examples to help you understand the differences:

- With stress, you worry about your bills, lack of a job, or getting dumped by your girlfriend. Once the stressor or trigger is taken away, you stop worrying. With an anxiety disorder, you are constantly worried about these things for no reason at all. You find yourself undergoing daily distress even though the stressor has disappeared.

- Stress is where you go to a social gathering and start feeling self-conscious or uncomfortable, maybe because of the way you are dressed. With an anxiety disorder, you totally avoid any kind of social gathering because you are afraid of being humiliated or embarrassed in some undefined way.

- Stress is what you feel before you sit for an exam, give a presentation, or attend an interview. A stressor is a significant event that can impact your life. Anxiety disorder, however, is where you experience a sudden overwhelming fear for no reason at all, and you live in perpetual dread having another panic attack.

- Stress involves a rational fear of what you consider a dangerous situation, place, or object. Once you leave the place or eliminate the threatening object, you become okay. With an anxiety disorder, you find yourself afraid of things that are non-threatening, and even though the object is removed, you remain terribly afraid.

- Stress is what you experience immediately after a traumatic event, for example, when you avoid a car collision. You may find it difficult to sleep after such a situation. However, an anxiety disorder is where you have recurring flashbacks or nightmares of the accident some months or even years after the event.

Experts are still learning more about anxiety disorders. They have found that it can actually run in families and has some sort of biological basis. So far, what we are sure of is that anxiety disorders are a result of a complex combination of risk factors that include genetics, personality, brain chemistry, and events you experienced in your life.

Chapter 2: Forms of Anxiety

There are a number of different forms of anxiety disorders, and some of them were mentioned in the previous chapter. In this book, we are going to focus on three of them: social anxiety disorder, panic attacks, and phobias.

Social Anxiety Disorders

Social anxiety can be described as the intense fear of being judged or scrutinized by people within a social setting. It is an anxiety disorder that causes extreme self-consciousness in normal social situations. You always feel as if everyone around you is watching your every move, and this makes you feel embarrassed by everything you do in public.

Social anxiety, which used to be called social phobia, usually starts before adulthood and can be so severe that it interferes with work or school life. People who suffer from this disorder are usually aware that their fear of being around others is excessive, but they simply don't know how to overcome it. If they have an upcoming social event, they will spend days or weeks worrying about it, and may even experience depression and low self-esteem. It is easy to assume that a person is just shy, but shyness and social anxiety are very different.

Social anxiety is linked to specific situations, especially those that involve public speaking or performances. It can be very difficult to maintain any kind of romantic or social relationships, and this compounds the problem by causing shame. You will only feel comfortable interacting with family members.

Symptoms

Physical symptoms of social anxiety include:

- Profuse sweating

- Blushing

- Trembling

- Nausea

- Difficulty speaking

- Mild stomach pain

- Rigid posture

- Rapid pulse

- Speaking too quietly

- Refusing to make eye contact

The worst thing about these symptoms is that they make you feel more self-conscious about yourself, thus generating a vicious cycle.

Causes

Ongoing research shows that social anxiety is caused by a tiny part of your brain known as the *amygdala*. This small structure is what controls your fear responses. Social anxiety is also passed down the family line. Other risk factors include childhood trauma and hormones.

Treatment

The good news is that social anxiety can be successfully treated if you consult a trained medical professional. There are a number of treatment options, but the most effective so far is cognitive-behavioral treatment (CBT) and specific medications. However, the most effective form of treatment so far has been CBT, which involves exposing you to the very thing that you are fearful about. You are introduced to the situation or object that makes you anxious and are then taught to handle the criticism or rejection that you normally disapprove of. We shall cover this in greater detail in one of the chapters ahead.

Panic Attacks

A panic attack can be described as a sudden onset of extreme fear that continually increases for a couple of minutes. When you have a panic attack, you just experience overwhelming fear and anxiety coming over you, but you may not really understand what is happening.

You feel as if you are about to die from a heart attacking due to the accelerated heart rate and other intense symptoms. However, you are experiencing the attack because of some psychological factors. A panic attack usually lasts for about 15 to 20 minutes, so the most important thing to do is to ride it out and wait for your body to go back to normal.

You may think that panic attacks are rare, but the truth is that they are quite common, with women being more susceptible than men. Though it is possible to experience a panic attack at any age, the majority of people tend to start feeling the effects between the ages of 25 and 30.

Symptoms

For you to be considered to be suffering from a panic attack, you must experience four or more of the following symptoms:

- Sweating

- Heart palpitations (increased heart rate)

- Trembling

- Shortness of breath

- Choking sensations

- Chest pain

- Feeling chilly or hot

- Light-headedness

- Abdominal discomfort

- Feeling like you are losing control

- Fear of dying

- Tingling or numb sensations

Causes

A panic attack is primarily the result of the adrenaline hormone flooding the body due to perceived danger. Notice that the key word here is perceived, which means that the problem is psychological in nature. As your adrenaline levels increase, you experience the above symptoms, but the hormone cannot stay at that high level for long, and soon drops down to normal.

Other factors that may contribute to your panic attacks include drinking too much coffee, stress, or failure to get adequate sleep. The best thing you can do is to try to figure out what triggered the attack in the first place. Maybe it was an impending exam or bad news about a loved one's health. Knowledge the cause will help you know what factors to avoid and reduce your anxiety about experiencing an attack when you least expect it.

Treatment

There are a number of recommended solutions for managing the symptoms of your panic attacks. They include taking slow breaths, distracting yourself by listening to music or watching TV or breathing into a paper bag. You can also use relaxation techniques like deep breathing, mindfulness, progressive muscle relaxation, and even exercise. Psychological treatment usually involves cognitive-behavioral therapy. We shall go deeper into some of these treatment options in the chapters ahead.

Though there are some who experience one or two attacks with no recurrence, I must inform you that you have to get a check up just to determine what the problem could be. If you leave the condition unaddressed, you may graduate from having panic attacks to developing a panic disorder. A panic disorder is where you have multiple panic attacks every month, and then you become deathly afraid of getting more attacks. You may end up developing what is referred to as agoraphobia, which is the fear of wide, open spaces that don't seem to have any escape route.

Phobias

A phobia is simply a severe irrational fear of a situation or object, even though there is no actual threat. Let's say you live in a 20-storey apartment block, but you are so afraid of falling off the building that you never go out onto the balcony to enjoy the view. Maybe you encounter a tiny spider that you know isn't poisonous, but you simply freak out and become anxious. These are examples of phobias.

Phobias are very common in most people so there's no reason to feel ashamed. However, if the fear stays with you for more than six months and prevents you from enjoying your daily life, then it becomes a psychological issue. If you have been living in your 20th-storey apartment but have never set foot on the balcony due to fear of falling off, you definitely have a phobia.

Symptoms

Phobias are characterized by severe fear every time you come into contact with an object or experience a particular situation. There are times when the mere thought of the object will trigger physical symptoms, such as:

- Lightheadedness

- Choking sensation

- Trembling

- Cold or hot flushes

- Vomiting

- Accelerated pulse rate

- Sweating

- Numbness

- Shortness of breath

- Tight sensation in the chest

- Feeling detached from your body (out-of-body experience)

If you recognize these symptoms, you may be suffering from a phobia. On the other hand, there are times when these symptoms may become severe, thus leading to a panic attack. Such an acute fear can make you feel embarrassed in public and make you withdraw from any situations that may bring you face-to-face with your fear. Though avoidance is one strategy, it will simply make the fear worse, and impact your life negatively.

Types of phobias

Phobias can be categorized into:

1. Specific phobias – As the name suggests, this is where you are afraid of one thing, for example, spiders. They start when you are a child but dissipate as you age.

2. Complex phobias – These are much worse than specific phobias because they develop in your adult life and disrupt your normal functioning. They are classified into social phobias and agoraphobia, both of which we have covered already.

Causes

As far as research is concerned, your phobia isn't the result of a single factor. There are several things that may have been responsible. They include:

- Specific trauma - For example, extreme turbulence on a plane during childhood may cause a fear of flying.

- Childhood environment – Your parents may have been overly anxious or constantly fearful, and you learned to respond in the same manner.

- Genetics

- Long-term stress

- Panic responses

Treatment

If possible, identify the specific causes of your phobia and face them head on. You can also seek professional help and use recommended techniques to address the phobia. Therapists will usually use cognitive-behavioral therapy to help you manage your phobia. There are also relaxation techniques such as stretching, controlled breathing, and meditation that can be very effective. Practicing mindfulness is also a good solution. Check out the coming chapters for more details on some of these techniques.

Other treatment options include joining a support group where you meet fellow sufferers and share your experiences and coping strategies. These groups can either be online or in person.

Chapter 3: Cognitive-Behavioral Therapy

Cognitive-behavioral therapy (CBT) is considered to be one of the most effective forms of psychotherapy in the treatment of anxiety disorders. The goal of CBT is to reduce your anxiety levels by helping you eliminate those negative beliefs that are making you feel fearful.

For example, if you are afraid of a particular object or situation, you are likely to avoid it. Maybe you feel anxiety when in large groups of people or are afraid of flying. Due to such fears, you will avoid public speaking opportunities or travel by plane. However, by avoiding the situation, you also lose the opportunity to see just how harmless it really is.

This is what CBT is all about. The key aspect of this psychotherapy is to expose you to the same thing that you fear the most, and this technique is referred to as *exposure therapy* or *desensitization*. You are shown how to confront your fears instead of running away from them. This is how you strip your fear of its power over your life.

There are three stages in the CBT process:

1. You are introduced to the object of situation that causes your anxiety. This is done in a safe and controlled environment. For example, if you have a fear of flying, you may read a magazine about planes, look at photos of people flying in a plane, sit in an airport lounge, or talk to pilots.

2. Your risk for disapproval in a particular situation is increased. This is done to help you build confidence and be able to handle criticism and rejection. In other words, you are exposed to more of whatever situation

you are afraid of. If you are afraid of going out and mingling with strangers, you will be asked to meet strangers and face your fear. The goal is to show you that you are strong enough to handle any potential criticism or rejection from others.

3. You are taught how to cope with disapproval. You are asked to visualize your worst fear and then come up with constructive responses on how to deal with the fear.

This process needs to be done by a professional therapist, and CBT is usually accompanied by other techniques, for example, deep breathing. Nothing is done without your permission, so you don't have to worry about being forced to do anything.

CBT has no negative side effects apart from the temporary increase in your anxiety levels as you face your fears. The treatment generally lasts for 12 to 20 weeks and can be done in groups or individually.

In the next chapter, we look at some simple techniques that you can do at home by yourself.

Chapter 4: Alternative Treatments

In this chapter, we are going to cover some alternative therapies that are also very effective in treating anxiety disorders. Unlike CBT which requires a medical professional, these techniques are simple and you can handle them on your own. These alternative therapies are also sometimes used in conjunction with CBT.

Relaxation Exercises

There are many ways in which you can relax. Some people play sports, exercise, listen to music, or read a book. On the other hand, others choose the option of relaxation exercises to relieve their anxiety. In this section, we will learn about two techniques that are very effective in combating the physical symptoms of anxiety. They are deep breathing and muscular relaxation.

Deep breathing exercises

One of the symptoms of an anxiety disorder is rapid breathing. This can lead to dizziness, which causes more anxiety and even faster breathing. It's a vicious cycle. By practicing how to breathe deeply when you are relaxed, you will be ready to do the same thing when anxiety strikes.

The important thing is to practice every day for about 3 minutes until it becomes normal for you. Deep breathing can also reduce any background anxiety you may have at any given time. Follow the steps below:

- Take slow and deep breaths through the nose and exhale through your mouth. Maintain a steady rhythm. Make sure that your breathing out takes twice as long as your breathing in. For example, if you breathe in for a count of two, breathe out for a count of four.

- Try to breathe from your diaphragm. Whenever a person becomes anxious, they tend to breathe from the chest rather than deep from the stomach. This means that you are practicing shallow breathing, thus resulting in shortness of breath.

- Place your hand below your sternum to check whether you are breathing from your diaphragm. You should feel the top of your abdomen moving in and out every time you breathe.

- When you breathe, make sure that your upper chest and shoulder muscles are relaxed. As you exhale, relax these muscles until you learn how to rely only on your diaphragm when breathing.

Muscular relaxation

This technique can be performed either as part of a planned program or at any time of the day.

For planned times:

Find a place that is warm and quiet with no distractions. Make sure you don't have any other urgent work that may interrupt you. You can either lie on your back or sit on a comfortable chair. Please read the instructions first to the end before you start doing anything.

You are going to work on different muscle groups with your eyes closed. You will first place the muscle under tension as you inhale, and then relax the muscle as you exhale.

To begin, focus on your breathing for a couple of minutes and then start.

- Hands – Breathe in as you clench the right fist for a few seconds until your forearm becomes tense; relax the muscle as you exhale. Repeat for the left hand.

- Arms – Breathe in as you bend your elbow and tense the muscles in your right arm; relax the arm as you exhale. Repeat for the left arm.

- Shoulders – As you inhale, raise your shoulders as high as possible. Exhale as you lower them.

- Face – Frown as hard as possible and lower your eyebrows for a couple of seconds; then relax the facial muscles. Raise your eyebrows for a few seconds and then relax. Clench your jaw and then relax.

- Chest – Breathe deeply for a couple of seconds and then revert to regular breathing.

- Buttocks – Clench your buttocks together as hard as possible and then relax.

Repeat this entire process 4 times every day and you will soon notice that your overall tension is reduced.

For everyday life:

Since you cannot do the above exercises when out and about, you may need some simpler techniques that can be performed anywhere. Use these techniques when you feel anxious:

- Turn your neck in both directions as far as possible, and then relax.

- Tense your back and shoulder muscles fully for a few seconds and then relax.

Mindfulness

This technique emphasizes being present in the moment. You don't worry about what will happen in the future and you don't reminisce about negative past events. Worry and thinking too much are two features of anxiety, which is why mindfulness is such a great strategy.

Follow these simple steps:

1. Sit in a comfortable chair with your neck and head supported. Make sure you are in a quiet place.

2. Set an alarm to go off after 30 minutes.

3. Close your eyes and pick a point of focus. This can be a mantra (for example, "everything is OK"), or you can focus on your breathing. Most people prefer focusing on breathing because it is rhythmic and constant.

4. Spend the next one minute easing yourself into awareness. Allow your mind to settle. You will start to notice sensations and other things trying to distract you but simply ignore them.

5. If breathing is your point of focus, pay attention to the way air moves into your nose, fills your lungs, and expands your abdomen. If your mind wanders, refocus back onto your breathing.

6. When your mind wanders, don't judge the thoughts and emotions. Just allow them to flow through without getting caught up in them. Bring your focus back.

7. Every time your mind loses focus, bring it back onto your point of focus. This may sound repetitive but the

truth is that your mind is always wandering all over the place, more so for anxiety sufferers. Mindfulness is a skill that you have to continuously practice and develop.

Confronting your fears

Many people are unsure of what drives their panic and anxiety. If you do have recognizable triggers, it can help to confront them head on.

People often feel embarrassed about their feelings and believe that friends, family and work colleagues will think they are crazy. These feelings cause them to try and hide what is happening to them. If this seems familiar to you, try to realize that by doing this you are doing yourself an injustice in two ways. Firstly, you are putting limitations in your life, which will cause you to miss out. Having fun is really important and it can play a big part in helping you to recover from anxiety. Secondly, you are removing potential "helpers" and "confidantes" who could be of great support to you when you are in need of a person to talk to.

Having trusted people that you can turn to and talk with during an attack can be beneficial to many people. Your confidante isn't there to advise you, if fact, they don't even need to say anything at all, they are there to listen to you. If you can talk about how you are feeling, describe your anxiety to them, vocalize it and allow yourself to break it down, it can help to alleviate the stress significantly. It also enables you to regain control of your emotions more quickly and easily than if you just tried to do it on your own.

Ideally, you should have several turn-to people that you can use as confidantes. They will need to be people you trust and feel safe with and who you feel won't be judgmental. People tend to be judgmental when they don't understand. Explaining to them what you are going through can make them a powerful ally against your anxiety. To see if they would mind being a confidante, you will need to ask their permission. Explain the role to them, so they understand they are only required to listen to you and not to advise you. Try to find people that are available wherever you are. So, a family member at home, a friend or colleague at work and so on. If they can be with you, face to face that is fantastic. If not, having them available on the phone will also work fine. That way you know there is always someone available to talk to.

Don't think that you are alone. Almost everyone at some point experiences anxiety. They may not have experienced panic attacks in the way you do. But they will understand how anxiety can be distressing.

Unfortunately, panic attacks don't always happen at home. They can occur anywhere and, in those situations, it is impossible to employ some of the other treatments that have been described. You can try the method described below to regain control when you are out and about.

When you are experiencing a panic attack, you often feel the urge to run away. This is your primitive fight or flight mechanism taking control. There are several things you should try to stop doing during a panic attack as they can exacerbate the situation and prolong the attack. If you want it to stop quickly so you can regain control fast, try the following:

- **Stop running away.** Fully accept that you are having a panic attack, that running away from where you are or who you are with is not going to change it. Remember, the panic attack cannot hurt you. It is just your primal fight or flight mechanism being triggered.

- **Stop using "coping strategies."** They are usually not effective when you are out and about. Instead of trying to find distractions, turn towards and embrace the feelings you are having. Realize that they cannot hurt you. Yes, they are unpleasant, but they cannot harm you and the more you accept them, the less powerful they become.

25

- **Stop the "what if" thinking**. What if this happens, what if that happens? None of it is actually going to happen. You are not going to die.

- **Stop conditioning future fear**. If you fear having future panic attacks, then you are actually going to cause them to happen through your fear. This is part of the vicious circle of cause and effect. Instead, learn to change your mindset. Rather than constantly worrying about when you will next have a panic attack, accept that it will happen but that it actually doesn't matter. Embrace panic attacks without fear. Accept them and allow them to ride out, knowing they cannot hurt you.

By accepting and embracing panic attacks, you take away their power. Remind yourself regularly that they are not dangerous. Anxiety is uncomfortable yes, but it is not going to kill you. The more you fear them, the more they will occur. Fear simply fuels panic attacks. Learn to be comfortable with your discomfort during an attack. Accept that what you are feeling is a normal response to your fear.

When you have practiced this and understand the mechanism, change your thought process completely. Now start to meet your fear, anxiety and panic head on. You can now start to dare a panic attack to happen, embrace it encourage it. By doing this, you will totally remove its power. If you feel panic rising, encourage it to happen. Face it and say, "Okay, bring it on." You will find that instead of becoming worse, the panic will quickly fade and actually goes away.

Magic Circle

Many people who experience panic attacks find that going to a "safe place," a specific room in their house, a cupboard or hiding under the covers of their bed, for example, can help to make them feel more secure. You can actually create the same safe feeling by making your own transportable safe place. This is called a "magic circle" It is simply an imagined circle of energy you visualize being around you, like a see-through wall of protection. You will need to really practice visualizing it, a wall of powerful energy moving around you. See the energy moving, protecting you. See the direction it moves in. Give it a color that you find soothing and strong. Give it texture. This circle of energy empowers you, protects you, and makes you strong. When you have really practiced visualizing the magic circle around yourself, you will be able to take it with you wherever you go. You can use it to make yourself feel strong, powerful and protected in any situation. This is useful when you find yourself places that can trigger panic attacks. Just visualize your magic circle and believe in its ability to keep you safe.

Diet and Exercise

You must realize that a poor diet and lack of exercise can aggravate the symptoms of anxiety. In most cases, a panic attack is preceded by an urge to eat something sugary, which is the body's way of telling us that blood sugar levels are low. This is why breakfast is such an important part of anxiety treatment. After 8 or so hours of fasting, you need to eat something to get your blood sugar back up again.

There are some foods that make anxiety symptoms worse. They include caffeine, alcohol, sugary snacks, and fizzy drinks. You should also avoid smoking, tranquilizers, and anti-depressants. The worst of all these is caffeine because it keeps you hyper-alert and makes you more vulnerable to panic attacks. Avoid chocolate, cola, tea, and cocoa.

You also need to drink enough water to ensure your body doesn't become dehydrated. When the body becomes dehydrated, the mind interprets this to be a threat to your survival, thus triggering a stress response.

An imbalance of minerals and vitamins can also exacerbate feelings of anxiety. It is a really good idea to ensure that you are getting enough of the vitamins and minerals that help your mental state.

You can try mineralizing your water by using pink Himalayan salt. Himalayan salt contains more than 84 minerals and trace elements such as magnesium, calcium, iron, copper and potassium, all of which our body needs to stay healthy. A special mineralizing liquid is known as "Solé" can be made using pink Himalayan salt. A small amount of Solé is added to the water you drink each day, which mineralizes it, making it easier for your body to absorb the minerals it needs.

To make Solé you will need the following:

- A ½ gallon glass or ceramic container with a tight fitting lid.

- High quality pink Himalayan salt from Pakistan (the only country to produce true pink Himalayan salt).

- Enough purified fresh drinking water to fill your glass or ceramic container.

All you need to do is:

- Add 2 tablespoons of the Himalayan salt to the water and allow it to dissolve for 24 hours.

- Simply add 2 teaspoons of the Solé to every 16 ounces (1/2 liter) of water you drink.

There are several minerals that play a key role in maintaining good mental function. A deficiency in them can cause quite dramatic differences in your mental wellbeing, so ensuring you are getting enough of them is really important for good brain function and mental health. These minerals include:

- Zinc. Can be found in oysters and pumpkin seeds. Or you can try making a zinc boosting smoothie by combining organic carrots, apples, spinach and a small amount of fresh root ginger.

- B Vitamins. You require a minimum of 25mg per day. They can be found in oily fish, such as trout or salmon. In lentils, brown rice and dark leafy greens.

- Folic acid. This helps with balancing your dopamine, serotonin and adrenaline release. Folic acid can be found in leafy greens, citrus fruits, legumes, brown rice.

- Calcium & Magnesium. These can be found in legumes, lentils, dark leafy greens, nuts and seeds.

Try to eat as healthy a diet as possible. Due to our busy lifestyles, it can be difficult always to ensure we are getting sufficient nutrients in our diets. This is why supplementing with really high-quality supplements can be very beneficial. That way you can be sure that your body is getting all of the minerals and vitamins it needs. Here, quality really does matter, as not all supplements are made equal. Ask your health food store for advice on choosing the best ones that are fully bioavailable and can be used by your body.

Exercise is also beneficial for protecting against anxiety and depression. Whenever you are anxious, your body produces adrenalin, but since there is no real danger, the hormone stays in the bloodstream without any use. By exercising, you utilize the excess adrenalin and minimize your anxiety symptoms. Working out also produces endorphins, which put you in a good mood.

Conclusion

Thank you again for downloading this book!

I hope this book was able to help you to learn more about anxiety and finally understand how it affects your life.

The next step is to take the action steps that are outlined in this book. Anxiety does not have to control your life. You have the power to handle whatever anxieties life throws at you by choosing to use the techniques described in this book.

We hope that you are now in a stronger position to overcome any anxiety disorder you may have.

Finally, if you enjoyed this book, then I'd like to ask you for a favor, would you be kind enough to leave a review for this book on Amazon? It'd be greatly appreciated!

Go to: **https://tinyurl.com/y7w9eezd**

Thank you and good luck!

FREE Ebook! Got to:

https://tinyurl.com/y9b98nfw

"Are You Feeling Stressed, Overwhelmed And Are Full Of Anxiety? If So Then We Have The _FREE_ E-Book That Gives Help On Getting Rid Of Your Stresses And Helps You Get On With The Rest Your Life!"

Stress Is The Number One Cause of Medical Problems In The United States Today. Anxiety Just Adds To Those Problems. But You Don't Have To Suffer Anymore! We Have The Answers You're Looking For!

Life today can be overwhelming – there's no denying that! Stress and anxiety can seem to take over our lives and render us helpless. It's easy to get caught up in all the drama and let those stressors dictate how we live. **Believe me, I know**!

I personally have dealt with an anxiety disorder that was aggravated and brought on by excessive stress. This illness has debilitated me for years leaving me ill-equipped to deal with even
the smallest problem. That is, until I figured out how to manage my stress and anxiety.

It will be an ongoing struggle for me, but the first step was learning how to cope with stressful situations that could bring on my anxiety. I had to spend a lot of money on doctors and

therapists
to get those tools that would enable to live a *fulfilling life.*

The good news is that if you are suffering from anxiety and excessive stress, you won't have to spend the same amount of money I did just to deal with my daily stress. You can get all the information you need – right here in this amazing book, **"<u>Eliminating Stress and Anxiety From Your Life</u>**"!

Unfortunately This Can Affect Everyone

Everyone has stress. It's a fact of life. How we react to that stress can make a world of difference, though. It can literally make us healthy or unhealthy.

Studies show that stress and anxiety contribute to at least 80 percent of all illnesses that people suffer from today. Over 19 million people are negatively affected by stress related disorders, but they don't have to be. There are ways that you can make stress disappear
or even work FOR you instead of *AGAINST* you.

Have you ever wondered how in the world you can manage the stress you feel? **Wonder no more** – we have compiled an amazing amount of information that will allow you to leave the stress behind and begin living a more fulfilling life – stress free!

When you order our **<u>FREE</u>** ebook, "**<u>Eliminating Stress and Anxiety from Your Life</u>**", you will get a combination of expert advice from psychologists, educators, and people who suffer from excessive stress and anxiety. They can give you many, many tools to make your life easier and let
you know what it's like to escape from the daily problems that can plague us.

Today, there are millions of people who suffer from too much stress. Stress causes anxiety. Anxiety causes health problems that can be debilitating. There's absolutely no reason why you have to suffer anymore. We're giving you the cure!

With This Incredible Book, You Will Learn:

- The difference between stress and anxiety

- How to recognize and deal with a panic attack

- **Using visualization to overcome stress**

- Letting music get rid of your anxiety

- And so much more!

  Not only will you get information about the stress and anxiety that can affect your life, you'll also get valuable advice and tips on how to combat that stress and take back your life!

  ## We Give You Over 25 Ways To Relax And Live a More Fulfilling Life.

  You'll learn:

- Self-hypnosis to relax

- How to tell people "No" when you should

- How to relax at work

- Ways to take a break that will renew your spirit

Stress is all around us and will always be a part of our lives. You need to be more resilient and pro-active when coping with your stress in order to be a calmer, happier person. Which is exactly why you need to order this book.

To get your FREE Ebook go to:

https://tinyurl.com/y9b98nfw

Check Out More Great Content! Click on the Cover for more info

Search: emotional intelligence Andrew on amazon.com

Search on Amazon: intermittent fasting andrew

(Preview Below) Search on Amazon: NLP andrew

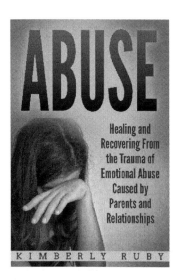

Search on Amazon: abuse Kimberly Ruby

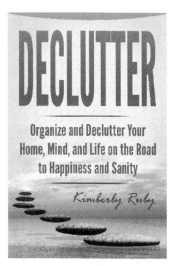

Search on Amazon: declutter Kimberly Ruby

Preview Of 'Neuro-Linguistic Programming: Techniques to Communicate to Your Inner Self and to Control Your Destiny'

Chapter 2: Improve The Way You Talk To Yourself And Believe In Yourself

One major reason why we feel unsure about ourselves or why we cannot live a life we actually want or why we doubt ourselves when others tell us we cannot do something is because we do not talk nicely to ourselves and do not believe in ourselves. When we keep saying mean things to ourselves or keep reminding ourselves of our past failures or mistakes, we are likely to think negatively. This is exactly what shapes a negative inner program that keeps creating more hurdles for us.

If you wish to live life on your term, you need to train yourself to talk positively to yourself at all times so you can slowly let go of the inner critic rooted inside you that makes you think negatively at all times. Here is how you can do that.

Calming The Inner Critic To Develop Positive Self-Talk

Your self-talk refers to the way you talk to yourself and can be both, positive and negative. If you keep saying negative and mean things to yourself repeatedly, you will train your mind to think negatively at all times which will turn your self-talk into a negative one.

This negative self-talk gives birth to your inner critic which is the annoying voice inside you that fires up every time you think of doing something. For instance, if you plan to take a workshop on communication skills, that voice will say something like 'What use will that workshop be to you? You are quite likely never to implement those teachings in your life because you are a failure.' Alternatively, if you plan to pursue your dream of becoming a guitarist, your inner critic is likely to remind you of the slip-ups you have had in life so you become demotivated. This happens because you have trained your mind to think a certain way.

To do what you wish to do and to feel self-confident, you need to learn to communicate in a realistic and positive manner to yourself so you build positive self-talk and slowly eliminate the inner critic from your mind. It won't go away completely because there is a part of our mind that is designed to make us doubt things and this is important so you can analyze dangers on time and steer clear of them. However, with this strategy, you will learn to control and minimize your inner critic, and think optimistically. Here is how you can do that so you can talk to your inner self, make yourself behave the way you want to and control your destiny.

- Sit somewhere quiet and think of anything that has been disturbing you for some time or anything you would like to pursue but haven't been able to do so because of your inner critic. For instance, if you wish to start your own online business, but your inner faultfinder keeps telling you that it will fail, address that issue.

- Tell yourself that you plan to start your own business and then analyze what your inner critic tells you. Whatever your inner critic says, do not shun it and acknowledge it. If it says, 'I don't think I can do it because I did venture into a business before too but it failed miserably', then thank your inner critic for bringing that to your awareness and then ask yourself positive questions.

- Ask questions such as 'Was there a time in my life when I did do something I wanted?' or 'Have I successfully done anything?' Asking yourself such questions encourages your mind to think of times when you did do something successfully and when you do come up with an answer, you can use it as a proof to show your inner critic that while you may have failed at a business, you can do stuff successfully if you keep trying.

- Use this proof to create a realistic suggestion to respond to your inner critic. You could say something like, 'Yeah, I did fail at a business before, but I can do things successfully so I guess if I try and work hard, I can make this venture a successful one too.'

- Your inner critic is likely to feel a bit surprised by this response, but it will say something in return. You need to keep having a realistic and positive dialogue with it so you keep silencing it with every response. Continue with this exercise for about 15 minutes and in a little while, you will feel you have somewhat conquered your inner critic.

- Make sure to practice this strategy every time your inner critic has something nasty to say to you and within a few weeks, you will train your mind to unconsciously think positively so whenever doubts bubble up inside you, your subconscious will automatically replace them with positive suggestions.

With time, you will get better at this practice and will become optimistic as well.

In addition, you need to practice positive affirmations to rewire your brain to think exactly the way you wish it to think and believe. This further helps you talk positively to yourself and constantly believe in yourself. The next chapter tells you how to do that.

To   get   book,   go   to:
https://tinyurl.com/y7xv59xn

Made in the USA
Middletown, DE
23 August 2020